IF ONLY THE SEA COULD SLEEP:
LOVE POEMS

D0556964

THE MARJORIE G. PERLOFF SERIES
OF INTERNATIONAL POETRY

This series is published in honor of Marjorie G. Perloff
and her contributions, past and present,
to the literary criticism of international poetry
and poetics. Perloff's writing and teaching have been
illuminating and broad-reaching,
affecting even the publisher of Green Integer;
for without her influence and friendship,
he might never have engaged in publishing poetry.

If Only the Sea Could Sleep:
Love Poems

Adonis (Ali Ahmad Sai'd)

Edited by:
Mirène Ghosssein and Kamal Boullata

Translated from the Arabic by Kamal Boullata,
Susan Einbinder and Mirène Ghossein

GREEN INTEGER
KØBENHAVN & LOS ANGELES
2003

GREEN INTEGER
Edited by Per Bregne
København/Los Angeles

Distributed in the United States by Consortium Book
Sales and Distribution, 1045 Westgate Drive, Suite 90
Saint Paul, Minnesota 55114-1065

(323) 857-1115 / http://www.greeninteger.com

First Published by Green Integer in 2003
English language translation ©2003 by Mirène Ghossein and Kamal Boullata
The original poems appeared in *Al-A'mal al Shi'riyya* (Beirut: Dar al-'Awada, 1971).
Original poems ©1971 by Adonis (Ali Ahmad Sai'd).
Published by agreement with the author.
Back cover copy ©2003 by Green Integer

Design: Per Bregne
Typography: Kim Silva
Photograph: Photograph of Adonis

LIBRARY OF CONGRESS CATALOGING IN PUBLICATION DATA
Adonis [Ali Ahmad Sai'd] [1930]
If Only the Sea Could Sleep: Love Poems
ISBN: 1-931243-29-8
p. cm — Green Integer 77
I. Title II. Series III. Translators

Green Integer books are published for Douglas Messerli
Printed in the United States of America on acid-free paper.

CONTENTS

Foreword

The poems gathered in this book come from Adonis's *Complete Works* (1971) and cover a span of thirty years. We chose them primarily because we like them, keeping in mind all the while our desire to give readers a comprehensive introduction to his love poems. The order in which they appear in this collection is not chronological.

For more than thirty years Adonis has been a very controversial poet, promoting unsettling ideas about poetry, politics, tradition and modernity, as well as religion, in an effort to keep the Arabic legacy alive through a constant reexamination of its tenets in the light of new developments. Here we present a more intimate aspect of his poetry, an aspect which tends to be overlooked in the debate that has surrounded his work and still does.

Throughout our work, Robert Frost's statement on poetry (that which is lost in translation) kept us awake. That and one essential question: Should we try to translate the words or their "effect," as Mallarmé would have advised. We tried anything that worked, giving priority to the Arabic text—except in a few cases, where we let the "intoxication" that permeates the text take over the accuracy of its translation. We also agreed that the untranslatable should be allowed to resist our efforts and come across as such, possibly awkwardly at times, rather than lose its identity.

K.B. & M.G.

Introduction

How does a reader of poetry respond to a love poem when he or she is surrounded by images (such an important part of one's referential system) that blur the boundaries between love and "Basic Instinct" and "Damage"? When "diamonds" are said to be a "woman's best friend"? When singing telegrams deliver messages of love by proxy? When valentine cards open up to emit a metallic "I love you." But if the divorce between *word* and *world* may complicate the reading, it also works in poetry's favor because it severs the connection with the familiar references and helps the reader concentrate on those the poem is trying to establish. The reader is forced to ask, what does the poem tell us about love? And what referential system, if any, does it create?

The first two poems in section one, *Early Poems*, can be seen as an unsteady beginning, chosen primarily for their chronological place within this collection. The first poem, "Love," evolves around a speaking voice, around "the living" and "the dead," and a series of objects which "love" the speaking voice. In both "Love" and the second poem, "The House of Love," the reiteration of the word "love" stresses the poems' inability to convey feelings of love, to do what love does. The poems' reality remains ideal in a truly romantic fashion.

The third poem in section one, "A Mirror for Khalida," reflects a transition in the poet's use of I and You. It establishes the identity of You as source of inspiration and as mentor: "Khalida/a wave which taught me/that the light of stars/the face of clouds/the moaning of dust/are all but one should flower."[1] These lines contain the seed of what Adonis elsewhere calls the "breaking of barriers," a notion that his poetry increasingly will try to accomplish. But in spite of its intimate mood and beautiful imagery, "A Mirror for Khalida" also displays its romantic inability to make good on its words: its five parts are inscribed within the chronology of its descriptive mode. The poem fails to fuse the reader to the poem or to derail the intelligibility of the reading, in a "cheering of blood" or "a beat of cymbal." The poem does, however, establish a framework within which later love poems might evolve, a framework based on two mutually exclusive images: the mobility of the "wave" and the all-consuming and liberat-

---

[1] *al-Masrah wal-Maraya* (Beirut: Dar al-'Awada, 1977), p.484

ing "flame." Together these movements contain the seeds of beginnings.

In the thirteen poems in section two, *Beginnings*, Adonis breaks the barrier between the specific and the generic. He does this by expanding one specific image—the love of Qays for Layla—to several men and women who are engaged in a new understanding of the very word "beginning," as if all beginnings were indeed one "flower." The beginnings Adonis refers to are not about chronology but about the kind of love—personified by Qays' platonic love for Layla—that drives the lover insane when separated from the love object. This reference to the poetry and legend of Qays and Layla, a wave which goes back to the seventh century, is counterbalanced by its opposite: "The Beginning of Madness" establishes a link with Qays—another name for Qays is Majnun, which means "mad"—while giving the source of that tradition an extra dimension. "Sex" also "has the face of madness."

The poem "Beginning of Word" probes yet another aspect of beginnings. Its last line—"between you and me words gather/and blaze"—suggests that a lover's body (space) is both the annihilation of words (time) and their beginning (time/space). This and other similar ambiguities and contradictions are at the core of Adonis' poetry, something he does not deny: "my body is full of contradictions."[2]

In *Beginnings*, the "wave" of words and the "fire" of bodies, accompanied by a host of supporting images (including "sail," "flame," and "insomnia") establish a polarity which the poems do not attempt to resolve. Indeed, the tension between the two movements forms the very basis of the poems' existence and serves as a vehicle which propels the poetry forward. Even so, the wave is more discernible in its reiterated motifs than in the poetic motion that propels it forward, for it lacks the adequate space (in these short poems) to gather enough energy to build into a storm.

In the poems in section three, *Long Poems*, Adonis finds the kind of space he needs to turn waves into breakers. The first poem in the section, "Unintended Worship," is the easiest on the reader, in the sense that it is less likely to blur the referential line between word and world. The poem's chronological beginning, its specific details associated with verisimilitude (a quarter in Damascus, a house, a landlord) starts a narrative only to be stopped by

---

[2] *Mufrad bi sighat al-jam'* (Beirut: Dar al-'Awada, 1977), p.176

a passion that "sweeps over" the poem "like fire." Qays revisited. But Qays' platonic obsession here becomes an intensely sexual experience where the lovers' bodies are "mingled" and "plowed" together, forming "a single field" of words where lovers "mumble" about "spices" and "thorns," and where they "harvest" in a "clamor" that resembles "the gentleness of the sea."

While Layla in "Qays" is perceived only through Qays' love for her, the woman lover in "Unintended Worship" has a voice of her own: "I am life/perish in me." The poem, whose beginning promises an ambiguous "mixture of possibilities," delivers it with a string of metaphors—woman-fire, woman-river, woman-flower, woman-city—a mixture whose common denominator is language, the "foundry" in which the poem's various registers are melted together into one reality: "Her body is his language, and with her body he speaks."

But what is a language's body? However tempting it may be to describe Woman as the embodiment of the poet's speech, the reader is only dealing with words. Each reader has his or her own understanding of the word "poem" and of a poem's "body." To this reader, a poem's body is that unique moment when language manages to make the reader aware of his or her own body by severing the referential link to the outside world—that is, by short-circuiting memory and its chronology of events. "My language, a single word: freedom," writes the poet. Unburdened, the reader's senses and feelings become free to connect with the poetry's movement and rhythm, to flow with a river's flow, to be lost in the "delirium" of "bodies" or "birds." The reader becomes an integral part of the creative process because he or she is helping "words" (like the poem's lovers) acquire "faces." Once free from chronology and referentiality, the reader can focus on what the poem is trying to do. In such moments, the barrier between text and reader, between understanding and feeling—like the "barrier" inside the "lover's skin"—vanishes and the poem functions as the poet intended. Words step out of the linguistic system, leaving a tiny hole in the intellectual understanding, a kind of unsettling lag.

The poem's references to Imru' al Qays (a chief representative of pre-Islamic poetry) link the poem to pre-Islamic poetry and some of its own concerns—space, desire, and rapture (*latha*), a beginning in its own right. This historical connection with Imru'al Qays is revitalized and expanded through the lover's own passion, its true poetic link.

"Unintended Worship" makes references to another historical figure, the thirteenth-century mystic Niffari. At first, the references to Niffari seem quite surprising in a poem of that nature, but one in particular offers a hint. The "cup of intoxication" may suggest that the poem, which focuses so intently on the intoxication of passion, sees the body as a source of intoxication in much the same way that mystics find intoxication by communing with God. The body, no less than God, is a "source of knowledge," derived from itself and not from the outside world. It too can "set free" the person, like a stasis *(waqfa)* which brings with it the all-consuming vision *(ru'ya)*. The poem proclaims that "breaking the barrier" between body and spirit is a far richer experience than keeping the two apart. "The body of the stayer dies," wrote Niffari, "but his heart does not die."[3] "Unintended Worship," however, claims that there is no need for any part of the person to die in the quest for ecstasy. On the contrary, the lover's passion invigorates everything it comes in contact with.

---

[3] Muhammad Ibn 'Abn al-Jabbar al-Niffari, *Kitab al-Mawaskif.* (London: Cambridge University Press, 1935), p.35. Note: "Stayer" is a literal translation of *waqif,* the person experiencing *waqfa.*

Although "Unintended Worship" makes no mention of the "heart" as we usually read about it in a love poem, the reader is by now familiar with a process of interchange and "mixture." The reader recognizes that words can be exchanged like lovers' "shirts," that the heart and "sex" are linked by desire—whether focused, diffuse, or "mingled"—and that both heart and "sex" contribute to one and the same pulse.

In this poem Adonis makes another important link with Niffari. According to the poet, the thirteenth-century mystic wrote History with his "heart's vision" and with "language's intoxication." If there is a rapprochement to be made between Niffari and Adonis, it should revolve around "vision" and "intoxication," to which Adonis adds the lover's physical passion. Even an Arabic History that has become stale with time, he implies, can be revitalized by passion and imagination.

The poem's references to history and literature bring to mind T. S. Eliot's essay, "Tradition and the Individual Talent," in which he shows that both disciplines can be revitalized by an individual, a new imagery that fuses modern and ancient. Adonis applies this, for example, to the woman-city of Damascus in section x, where he suggests that the passion for a woman/city might restore some of the city's memorable history, with the poetic body acting as the medium.

"Unintended Worship" is so vigorously "carried on the back" of passion that its last lines sweep the reader along in their upward movement, oblivious to the "absence" that precedes them: *Haihat*,[4] *haihat*/inhabited towards you/lost to you, entrusted to you by the wind."

The second long poem in this collection, "Transformations of the Lover," brings with it a sense of bewilderment (what is the poem about?), coupled with a feeling of having entered Alice in Wonderland. Like children, the poem has no problem with "dancing flowers" or a "walking" brook. Like them, it does not associate the snake with the ambiguous double symbolism of life and libido, one of the oldest archetypes of human iconography. Although the poem uses the word *thu'ban* for snake, the word has a more common synonym, *hayya*, which shares the same root with the word for life, *hayat*, and which, in its adjectival form, means "lively" and "vivifying." The wave, which in "Unintended Worship" revives history

---

[4] *haihat* is a concise and emphatic expression to say that something is utterly out of the question.

and a culture through passion, travels a vertical road in "Transformations" from the "deep" to the "sky."

To the reader who attempts a walk through the poem's "forest of letters," the road feels more like a clearing than a stroll. The poem is so densely populated with "tribes" of symbols, similes, metaphors, prosopopoeia, and other literary creatures that the reader feels lost at every turn. Is it because the poem's transformations have not "touched" the reader that the reader feels like an outsider? And in any case, what kind of transformation is the poem talking about?

"Liber, Libera, Phallus" and "Thus says the lord, the body"—these words, repeated throughout the poem, can be seen as its *leitmotiv*. The most obvious reading of "liber, libera" links male and female liberation to fecundity, represented by the phallus, a symbol of life. But *liber* is also Latin for "book," while *libera*, used at the beginning of the Roman Catholic prayer for the dead, would connect words and death through Shahrayar at the end of song VI, establishing a link between death and language, in which the latter is a shield against the former.

Because "Transformations" would require so much unraveling, I will focus on three points that also are at the center of all the poems in this collection: I, You, and

Body.

"I pleaded and realized I have no voice"—I, a speechless voice, "hanging from the tower of a dream." Dreams, according to Freud, shred the events of one's life into pieces so that they become unrecognizable to the conscious mind and, in their altered form, can be expressed without censorship. If "Transformations" takes the shape of a dream, it does so to set free "all that is captive." But the fragmentation of the poetic material is also a linguistic device that checks the mind's linear reading and opens the way to the imagination and the senses. By using a dream to create a referential basis for the poem, Adonis increases his control over the material, manipulating it like "a sorcerer": "I was reared in dreams and built upon them."[5] The reader's attention is diverted by the literary tricks, the fantastic imagery ("a breast dressed in buttocks"), and the many voices of persons and objects, so that the speaking voice becomes relegated to the background, as though it were "speechless."

"The body is estranged, transformation has touched it." The most obvious transformation in the poem relates

---

[5] Adonis, *Abjadia Thania*. (Casablanca, Dar Tukbal, 1994), p.139.

to chronology or, to put it differently, to the relationship between Time and Space. A reading of just the first page alerts the reader that Time, which we apprehend through the occurrence of a string of events, is being challenged by the poetic space at every turn. The fragmentation of perception that comes with the continuous shift in registers, the repeated displacements and the fairy-tale quality of many of the passages make the reader lose track of chronology and of his or her self—outside the poem's reality. The "intoxication" of a liberated language, "libera," seems contagious. After an especially bold image ("I saw an elephant emerge from the horn of a snail"), the emboldened reader may ask, which horn was it? The reader may even suggest that the poor elephant try a different exit next time, it looked so squashed.

The poet's sorcery, which keeps the reader distracted, also distracts the speaking voice from the burning "wound"—"the incandescent hell." The poet uses displacement ("displace my fixed stars") to subvert the order of things: "I hear strange words turning into gardens," he writes, instead of putting gardens into words. Speaking of the order of things, when was the last time you read the scriptures? "And I remembered Eve and Adam's rib and knew you were my wife." Or is Eve language, and therefore comes first? A woman is "written with the lover's pen." "The words are pregnant." *Whose baby?* "You bear fruit in me." *I thought the language was pregnant.* After several readings of "Transformations" the reader, who began as an outsider to the poem, discovers with delight that he or she is becoming an active partner in the reading. The transformation within the poem begins to work on the reader too.

"Transformations" often turns language into the subject of the poem. It is as though the "hearts" that were "a mirror of mine" have been replaced by words acting as mirrors. For example, the woman "written with the lover's pen" reflects all the women in the other poems, each poem contributing a specific "wave" (a word associated with every woman) to the concept of woman as language, the primordial wave that encompasses all women. In "A Mirror for Khalida," the concept of woman suggests the interchangeability of all elements (all "one flower"), as well as the image of a "cloth" or "garment" which covers and unites the lovers, and which the lovers exchange. In "Unintended Worship," the woman brings a lyrical and robust passion which "ignites" her lover and everything the lovers come in contact with. "Transformations" takes these concepts further than any of the other poems, developing the notion of woman as language, but also as object and subject of love. The many women, because of their syncopated and fragmented presence, make for intermittent reading, changing a fleeting vision of a woman. While pointing up the "distance" by which "the wound" separates these women, the fragmentation also highlights the linguistic form that brings them together.

The Poetics of "Transformations" is about the pulse of language rather than its horizontal and cumulative production. It is about the dazzling effect of a language that has been turned into its own metaphoric vernacular, with its built-in tensions and controversy. And it is about comparison, juxtaposition, contrast, and collision, and about their coexistence, in a poem where the barriers have crumbled. The result is a dense and richly textured poem, where the imagined, the symbolic, and the metaphoric all contribute to, strengthen, and expand each other. Transformation is about the kind of freedom that brings births and beginnings, about changing one's identity as if it were a shirt, and about self-confidence (would *you* give your "face" to a "street" and feel the same?). Most important, transformation is about the child-like sense of play that gives the poem its raison d'être. The poem is a kind of "game" which "shuns away from roots and keeps moving" and "gives each thing its mystery and its flux," rather than "glorify its roots" or "encircle itself in its identity."[6]

And yet, in the face of such linguistic prowess, the reader of "Transformations" is left with a lingering question: was the object allowed to exercise its freedom and put up a resistance? The kind of resistance that refuses to let the words say it because experience itself is speech enough? The kind of resistance that causes the speaking voice to falter, hesitate, and even sometimes relent its sorcery? "I am a sorcerer." If the linguistic sign can stimulate such overwhelming freedom and creative energy, what is the poem saying about that which is not inscribed in it, keeping in mind that the speaking voice is attracted to that which "exiles" it? Is the speaking voice, exiled from the world and building a substitute world of its own ("language is the only living and free space"[7]), freer than the world of political regimes and social institutions? Adonis elsewhere states, "I write in a language that exiles me."[8] One wonders whether this double exile is the rea-

---

6 Adonis, *Kitab al-Hisar* (Beirut: Dar al-Adab, 1985), p.227

7 Adonis, *al-Nass al-Kurani wa Afaq al-Kitaba* (Beirut: Dar al-Adab, 1993), p.87

8 ibid, p.13

son he chooses to dwell in the "distance—the wound," and chooses "the wind" and "madness"? One wonders, too, whether in the final analysis, poetry in its relation to the reader, is a "questioning leading to a continuous questioning."[9]

The last poem in this collection consists of excerpts from "Body," published in the volume called *Mufrad bi Sighat al-Jam'* ("Singular in Plural Form"). The opening lines of the poem introduce us to the concept of the "wound," one of the most important motifs in the whole of Adonis' corpus: "The earth was not a wound/it was a body."

The wound originates within the speaking voice: "I meditate and go berserk/something is lodged between me and me." This leads to the question: "How can I incite my body to overcome me?" The lines that follow suggest that the answer lies with the speaking voice, which once again turns to sex in an attempt to heal the split: "Two lips attack his inner thighs/repeating a history which repeats itself." From this vantage point, "He has a glimpse of eternity/he senses the beginning." And what is that

---

[9] ibid, p.15

"something lodged between me and me"? My favorite candidate is the Word, whose status in "Transformations" challenges that of the speaking voice, in the manner of a true sorcerer's apprentice. If the speaking voice can write that "objects have no names/objects have hips and faces like lovers,"[10] that "the object is the word,"[11] and that the speaking voice is "silence," then it is quite normal for words to acquire hands and "steal" the speaking voice's "face."

Another possible answer to the question comes from a passage in "Body," not included in this collection: "Under his complexion, demons to no end."[12] Trapped by demons "he is wounded," and "the wound began changing into words."[13] Where does the answer lie? Are we faced by a Baudelairian-type predicament, where the Word is both *plaie* and *couteau*?

But can language dislodge what is splitting the speaking voice, can language act as demon and healer? The answer given by "Body" comes in the form of yet another

---

[10] Adonis, *Mufrad,* p.147
[11] ibid, p.143
[12] ibid, p.62
[13] vol.2, p.696

wound, this time between two verbs, "to take" and "to reach." "I take you a land I do not know" is followed by a series of futile attempts that exhaust the possibilities of "taking" and only serve to enhance the rift between taking and knowing. But the various acts ("I take you in waking, in sleep—standing, sitting, reclining") focus on the acts rather than the goal. In many passages of "Body" we find beautiful metaphors of woman as nature ("heights wrapped in clouds oblivious of sun/ridges blazing with a sun oblivious of clouds")—reminiscent of a movie scene where the camera shifts from the lovers to a scene with breaking waves or a hurricane. We learn from taking that the act is not a single event but a string of interrelated ones each of whose reiterations blurs and abolishes the borders (here, between woman and nature), conjugating the attributes of real and unreal, and bringing together curves and colors, hills and time, in one tidal "wave" of words, all of which are annihilated by a single burning question: "Who are you?" The three words act like "fire," arresting the wave and the reader. And still the speaking voice, obstinate and seeking, continues: "I stretch in you, I do not reach/I circle yet do not reach I thread and weave myself and still I do not reach." But, one may ask, if "the journey is you," does the speaking voice want to "reach," or is it indeed merely "building roads which lead nowhere"?[14] The imagery suggests that love is not a goal the lover ever reaches, allowing the lover to relax and settle, but that it lies on the road whose most important feature is that it excludes an arrival.

The wound cutting across the whole of Adonis' corpus is the "wound/distance" that lies between experience and language, between "object" and "word" or silence and word, the wound of which all the other wounds that inhabit the corpus (biological, historical, cultural, psychological, social, and so on) are but circumstantial representations. This wound is a choice Adonis has consciously made: "Some write and live in the space which forever separates word and object. When it comes to poetry, I am happy to be one of them."[15] And when "the wound began changing into words," the words kept in touch with the wound, their source. This is the kind of wound that proves to be a positive influence, since it forces the speaking voice to travel the distance which separates and links, the only space that makes one's identity a plural.

---

[14] ibid, p.16
[15] Adonis, *al-Nass al-Kurani*, p.83

To live in the "space which forever separates" is to be forever transient while feeling the attractions of the two poles from which one is exiled. It is to acquire "features of masculinity and femininity"[16] and settle in the land of the ambiguous and the perplexing, unable to choose, able only to question. It is to consider the "wound" a "sign" of "crossings" and keep moving toward new poles. It is to make the wound a positive force instead of succumbing to the pain. It is to "wash one's self of one's own life/like a river/and know nothing save the source and the wandering."[17] It is to be "exhausted" and to wish, "If only the sea could sleep." It is to ask, "Who are you?"—you the speaking voice and you the poet—and "Who will tell Adonis who he is?"[18]

Who will tell a speaking voice something about its identity? If "words" have "stolen his face," they should be able to say something about it. Words are the only things the reader can explore—their "anger" and "caresses," their "rhythm" and "music." But within the poetics of transformation in these poems—where a speaking voice can

---

16 *Mufrad,* p.177
17 ibid, p.82
18 Adonis, *Mufrad,* p.330

"change" into an "ostrich"—which identity do these words reflect? If the "stone" is a "bud" and "the cloud" a "butterfly," whose features does the reader see? When "My face has passed into the street's face,"[19] is it fair for the street to have a hybrid face? When "words have stolen his face,"[20] is it fair for a face to lie flat on a page and look like letters? Unless, that is, words can acquire in the process the "face" of "lovers."

In "Transformations" the phallus symbolizes the creative process, which is linked to freedom. In "Body," however, the *leitmotiv* has shifted from the phallus to the sun, the source of light and life, and therefore also the source of reflection and questioning, "O sun! O sun! What do you want from me?" the speaking voice asks in "Body." But the reiterated question only brings more and yet more questions, leaving the reader with the impression that the primary subject of "body," as well as the poem, is questioning—about one's own identity, the other's identity, and the relationship between the two.

The "wave," the sea—a locus and a symbol of beginnings and transformations, of the multiple currents that

---

[19] Adonis, *al-Masrah wal-Maraya* (Beirut: Dar al-Adab, 1968)
[20] Adonis, *Abjadia,* p.138

spell constant movement in all directions, of life and death, which share the same poetic space. For Adonis the wave, which originates with Ishmael and Ras-Shamra, has brought with it a series of places and persons that continue to inhabit its pages. To Imru' al-Qays and Niffari, to Damascus and Marrakech, one can add Gilgamesh and Al-Mutanabbi, Whitman and Baudelaire, Thamud and New York, among a great many others. They come to us, not in their original settings and ways, carried on a wave, but making waves as if their course had been charted by Ishmael, the ancestor: "My ancestors are a passion for space."[21] "Are" ... "passion" ... "space." Is there a more challenging way to assert one's lineage than connecting with one's "ancestors" through passion, rather than imitation? A passion for one's own poetic space. That ancestral space which was so central to pre-Islamic poetry—transient, in the image of the society—with its built-in endemic wound and nostalgia for the space it so often had to leave. A space which needed to be replaced with one easy to pack, to carry, to keep; the space of nomads, of troubadours, of rug weavers. The space of poetry ("the

---

[21] Adonis, *Kitab*, p.228

body," "the fire"), where the "wave" (time) keeps pushing and moving forward.

"Love is inventiveness, energy, something which no single poem states but which pervades them all,"[22] writes Adonis in *The Qur'anic Text*. He also writes, "I have named language woman and writing love,"[23] anticipating the difficulty of reaching his goal. He has embarked on "breaking the barrier" between the two, through a repeated act which although endlessly repeated, is never able to "reach." Love, like the body, therefore bears an inherent wound, similar to that which connects body and language: There is an "essential link between the nature of language and that of the body, similar to that of melody and string."[24] Body ... language ... love—their identities are intermingled, "singular in plural form," and yet they form "a bridge" that the lovers "cannot cross" but which still "brings (them) together." There is no attempt at arrival because "roads" are only to be traveled.

The notion of Love we find in these poems is, by its

---

[22] Adonis, *al-Nass,* p.81

[23] Adonis, *Shahwat Tatakadam fi Kharait al-Madda* (Casablanca: Dar Tukbal, 1987), p. 8

[24] Adonis, *al-Nass,* p. 82

sheer being, an indictment of a society and a world where love as "inventiveness" and "freedom" has become a rare commodity, replaced by the routine, the fast, the easy, (which alleviate the questioning), and the ready-made, infinitely easier than the created and more apt to be consumed. But these poems are primarily about themselves, about a form which, like a "vessel," takes the shape of its love, forming a love retrospective that moves away from the word itself (as we see it in the early poems) toward its dynamics and meaning. ("*Et de la mer elle-même il ne sera question, mais de son règne au coeur de l'homme*"[25]). A retrospective that creates yet another wound between the time of innocence—where a young lover could tell his beloved "I love you, I love you"—and the all-encompassing time of love as an act of poetic creativity.

—MIRÈNE GHOSSEIN
NEW ROCHELLE
1996

---

[25] Saint-John Perse, *Amers* (Paris, Gallimard, 1957), p. 18

I. Early Poems

LOVE

The road and the house love me

The living and the dead

The red jug

At home

Its water in love with it

The neighbor loves me

The field and the threshing floor

The fire

The arms that toll

Happy with the world

or unhappy

the tear my brother shed

hidden by the crop

Anemone that mortifies the blood

I have been here as long as the god of love

What would love do if I died.

THE HOUSE OF LOVE
Excerpts

I love you

as if all hearts were a mirror of mine

as if life were invented for my love

I love you

O how much I deleted from your lips

built my heart into a road and a house

hung it as a cloud over clouds

and how I equated beauty with you and let fantasy sprout

and how and how

I love you

the light in your eyes has withdrawn

it has been flooded

your hair like drifts of snow poured on your shoulders

braided, tied or loose

I feel time has melted in my eyelids

solidified and tumbled

like silence.

1. The Wave

Khalida
A branch for twigs to leaf around

Khalida
A journey which drowns the day
In the water of eyes
A wave which taught me

That the light of stars
The face of clouds
The moaning of dust
Are all one flower...

2. Beneath the Water

We slept in a cloth woven

From the crimson of night—a night of nebula and guts

A cheering of blood, a beat of cymbals

A lightning of suns beneath the water.

The night was pregnant.

3. Lost

...Once

I got lost in your hands, my lips were

A fortress

Longing for outlandish conquests

In love with siege

You came forth

Your waist a sultan,

Your hands the vanguard of armies,

Your eyes, a hiding place and a friend.

We clung together, drifted, entered

The forest of fire—I outline the first step

You open the road.

4. Fatigue

The old fatigue my love

is blooming by the house

it has a drawer by now,

and a window.

It sleeps in its huts, and disappears.

O how we worried about its wandering, we ran

roaming the place

asking, praying

we sight it and scream: how, and where?

each wind

has come

each branch

but you did not...

5. Death

Then the little hours come

Steps and roads recur

Then the houses decay

The bed puts out the fire of its days and dies

as does the pillow.

II. Beginnings

QAYS

Qays used to say

    I have clothed my body with Layla

        and clothed the human race.

I saw him hide his face

        in fire

        basking in the wood's nocturnal friendship
        and dallying.

I saw him gathering the moon,

one handful after the other,

from the shores of

insomnia.

BEGINNING OF SPACE

The body of earth foretells fire,

water; its impending fate.

     Is this why winds turn into palm trees

     why space becomes a woman?

BEGINNING OF ENCOUNTER

A man and a woman:

within them a reed meets a sigh

rain meets dust

      mounds crumble

      and the stifled language catches fire.

I ask: which one of us is the impending cloud

And which the notebook of sorrow?

      Your eyes are wilderness

      your face hears no question.

I am the very end of night. I fall to love

    so I may launch the fall of night

and say

    a man and a woman

    have met

    a man and a woman.

BEGINNING OF THE NAME

My days are her name

The dreams, when the sky is sleepless
    over my sorrow, are her name
The obsession is her name
and the wedding, when slayer and sacrifice embrace
        is her name.

Once I sang: every rose
    as it tires, is her name
    as it journeys, is her name.

Did the road end, has her name changed?

BEGINNING OF THE WAY

Night was paper—we were
    ink:

"Did you draw a face, man, or a stone?"
"Did you draw a face, woman, or a stone?"

I did not answer   We loved

Our hush has no way
like our love, it has no way.

BEGINNING OF TRAVEL

Encounters come, the sun dips in them
encounters go, the wound opens in them
    I do not know the tree's branch anymore
    nor does the wind remember
    my features   is this my future?
the lover asked a flame.
Yearning for the journey rising in her face
he sailed in her.

BEGINNING OF LOVE

Lovers read the wound   We wrote the wounds

    into another time   We painted

    our time:

    my face was evening,

    your eyelashes the morning.

Our footsteps are blood and longing.

Every time they rose they plucked us,

hurling their love, hurling us,

a rose to the winds.

BEGINNING OF SEX-I

Room   balconies   darkness

    tracing of wounds

    a body breaks

       slumber

between wandering and loss

our blood revolves in question and answer

    speech is the maze.

BEGINNING OF SEX-II

Rooms bending in arms, and sex uplifting its towers—

                        thrown

    into a gulf of sorrow

           sorrow

    within a gulf of waists—and sex opening its gates—

    we entered.

Fire was growing and night huddled its lanterns

    we fashioned

    a mound, filled a pit

    and whispered to the far-reaching space

    to offer up its hands.

The light of bitterness was like a river

    its banks lost, we made

its water ours, we made

our own banks a garment

for the whims of the river's banks...

BEGINNING OF WORDS

Our two bodies   thunder

     you say, I listen

     I say, you listen, words mingle.

Our two bodies   an offering

     you fall, I fall

     fantasies and flares around us

     you fall, I fall.

Between you and me

     words gather

     and blaze.

BEGINNING OF WIND

"Body of night" she said, and continued "home
    for the open wounds and their days..."

We began as dawn begins, we enter the shadow
our dreams interlaced
and the sun loosens its buttons: "foam veiled by the sea
    shall come." We were
reading to ourselves our own distance.

We rose and saw the wind erase our traces
    we whispered
    we will resume our secret meetings
    and parted...

BEGINNING TO SPELL

Now we may wonder how we met
now we may decipher the road of return
    and say: seashores are abandoned
        and masts are
            news of a wreck.

Now we can bow and say
    we came to an end.

BEGINNING OF MADNESS

When your winds swept over his boundless forests

    he said: death has the shape of a butterfly

    and sex the face of madness.

There he is now, wearing what the sacrificial victim wears

    his tomorrow

    his yesterday

    his horizon

    a blade, and dust of words

        before his eyes.

III. Long Poems

I GIVE MYSELF TO THE ABYSS OF SEX
Excerpts

You were the desert and I jailed snow in you
like you I split into sand and mist
You were a god to whose face I cried to erase the semblance
between us, I said I merged your body with mine
You were the crack filled with my waves
I was the barefoot night when I admitted you
through my navel
You multiplied my footsteps into a road, you entered
into my innocent water.
Expand. Strike roots into my loss.

On my pleasure's ice I walk
between riddle and miracle
within a rose.

I slipped into your basin
an earth revolving around me, your limbs a flowing Nile/
we floated we sank
you crossed into my blood my waves crossed over your bosom
You broke. Let us begin: love has forgotten the edge of night
should I shout, flood will come?

Let us begin: a scream mounts from the city, people are
　　walking mirrors.
If salt goes by, we meet, will you?
　My love is a wound
my body a rose upon the wound to be plucked by death,
　　a branch　　surrendered of its leaves and settled.

I entered your basin holding a city beneath my grief
　　what transforms the green branch into a snake
　　the sun into a dark lover.

　　　　　We were fused into each other
　　　　　　　I heard your heartbeat
　　within my skin (are you an orchard?)
the barrier fell (were you a barrier?)
the seagull asked the thread woven by the sailor
　　the traveler's snow sang an invisible sun (are you my sun?)
the lost man heard a voice (were you my voice?)
my voice my lifeline your lustful pulse your breasts were
my darkness and every night was my whiteness.
A cloud rolled I surrendered my face to the flood
　　and stayed among my own remains.

In my passion you melted
No borders bound my senses no sword sweeps asunder...
We were both one face. My shirt is no apple nor you
a paradise. We are field and harvest guarded by
the sun. I made you ripen. Come forth from the
green edge. This is our plenty: our bodies are the sower and
    the reaper.
Only you are one with my limbs and organs
Come forth from that edge
I bespeak my own death.

You define your own skin
loosen your lips fuse them between my teeth
I am night and day a lull in time
in our fusion
strike roots into my loss.

UNINTENDED WORSHIP
Excerpts

I

...Hence, she was unintended worship, a mixture of
possibilities as he wandered in what seemed to be streets
and alleys in the quarter of *Naqqashat*
in *al-Qassa'*
reading the roots of history, heading towards a woman
who read the branches
"This is hers"
the landlord looked like a rainbow he once saw in a forest
"She will come tomorrow."
Greetings to that house
like a silent bell infiltrating the night
welcome to the poet
gone astray
like a star about to fall.

For a time
he has spoken of joy and grief
another chance to get to know her
another urge to feel beleaguered
he wavers in her and towering, he looks:

"Are you a part of my abyss, of my upheaval."
To me, to my stage, O scattered one
I am your unexpected
you are the one who vanquishes my insides
each of us a separate war.

Why is he only filled with the love he awaits
why doesn't this love come forth?

...Within a love yet to come, he draws his face on a cloud
and bequeaths his body to memory's shadows
life is a flute of dust
a willow of grief stretching to the horizon.
And above *Hamidia*, here are the stars seeking windows in
    Immigrant's Quarter
they extend their hands to *Kassiun*, leaving their thighs in some
    obscure beds
here is the city—a soldier of snow,
a hole in his left side, the rest is ours
it is History—an ailing horse, brackish water drippings form
    its hooves
sprout in the wound, O salt, like a stag's horns
hunger is birth
and the earth too narrow for the earth.
How should he read you, O woman/O City
how should he read you?

—his intentions? his goal?
—his goal is thunder/his intentions a flood.
...

Silence—
no sound save the breathing of the lungs
"mingled with you
I moan you
write you in every cell
utter you, O my language and yield."

"A reed leaning to you
a bit of grass you have intoxicated
scatter me over your features
I insert myself in you and say to my body,
you are plowed with his body
we are a single field now and I say
wait for me at the far end of the harvest
be my Autumn
Spring is nothing but a preface
Summer, nothing but thirst
Winter just waiting
—ripen me, O autumn-poet
since I cast off time like a wild river and scream: I am life
perish in me
ignite

you the rising above my eyes.

We inaugurate the kingdom of our bodies—I proclaim
I love you and push the body's limits away
I love you and grow in you, a bewitched plant
I love you and say your love exceeds me
I love you and say: "my love is the river
we will not cross the river twice" ...

II

...Hence
he was a tower of light, had the breadth of the horizon, he filled
    space with space, linked
time with time
she named him the lover who exiled her to himself
to herself. She whispered
"Adorn your body with him—he is lightning
come forth.
Challenge him, be assertion
    and versatility
Some of us are the other's sacrifice
each of us is the other's worship..."

III

He listens to her body (her body is his language, with
        her body he speaks)
he speaks of the journey between ink and paper
between limbs
speaks against...
speaks of upheaval of the body and of its power
speaks to establish a blood rule between their bodies
to make his writing worthy of her body
to remain at the height of death.

He thinks that ...
is it why the poet says:
I create—I create nothing but cracks and rifts?
Is it why he says to the woman—the city
I write in order to belong to you
my face a meteor
and you the space?

...And she asks her body: am I the secret of his knowledge
is it his meaning or his image which gravitates around me?
her body wrote:
say his face changed to dew drops trickling down the windows
say his face went out for a stroll with time
and here are tribes of grass
raiding the distance at his side

...Thus we proclaimed
we are the first two bodies and death our third
thus she used to write:
"time is dual, silence and speech
the speech—the body, death—the silence"
thus he used to read
"tailor, my love is torn—can you sew it for me?"
"only if you have threads of wind."

...Hence
there remains nothing for us but to love
not knowing why
there remains that which no power can grant
and no authority refuse:
my freedom to accept you and yours to yield.
I wear your shirt and attach myself to you
you wear my shirt and attach yourself to me
we beautify the skin of the earth
we sexualize the universe.

IV

...How do I read you read you O city/woman?
with such sweetness
you cut my body vein after vein
and all I can offer is a bit of happiness
a lot of grief.
Still I grant your children all my anger and strength
since I teach my life but a single road—the body—and tell
my language to be a single word—freedom.

V

...In a language teaching itself to become freedom
the poet asked the river *Barada*:
Barada, is there a single face left
which truly frowns when it frowns
which truly smiles when it smiles
a single face
with which to exchange
the instinct of stone and the veracity of wind?
...With an instinct of stone and veracity of wind
the night fashioned (while looking at the poet)
a star from a different generation, something like a violet
like a woman in love
to whom he clung.
His soul hates wars
yet his body loves destruction.
He used to mutter to himself:
the sky to the stars
the earth to the stones
    where do you fit, you who resemble me
you they call human?
...indeed, history thinks with its feet
and here it is, laboring to remain afloat from stone to stone
here it is perishing like stunned birds
hissing by locked windows
delirious and about to faint...

VI

...In what seemed to be the sobbing of a flower
she emerged from a basin of confusion into her destiny
crushed into musk between two lips, dripping onto her body
what a strange lover she is
a tree trunk would break in front of her
a flower would overwhelm her.
And here, he ignites for the second time
his fiery guts branch out into luxurious bushes.
What a strange lover he is: a tree trunk would break in front
    of him
a flower overwhelms him,
...his rituals are at stake,
and between what remains of *Imru'-al Qays*
the friend whose path leads to *Niffari*,
offering the cup of intoxication—
it is possible that hallucination has a halo
that tears have a circle of waves—a bed to carry us,
or a ship to drip our bodies.
It is possible that the flavor of two bodies may change into
    flocks of birds
going about the business of the wind
possible we will separate
and nothing will remain between our bodies but our bodies.

...Thus behave his limbs,
O you who named her "my love"
O woman, the addiction of his eyelashes...
Afterward, and if, and no matter what...

VII

...It was left to the sun's radiance to capture a woman's body
and ask:
how many centuries deep is your wound?
It was left to the pavement to welcome women
forests and forests
and leave the outcast to ambush the fleeting breasts...

VIII

A moment of lust a moment of pull
time the drunkard is intoxicated with your name,
    O woman/city
but my thirst is a solar oven, and your eyes have no sisters.
O abyss
which passion relays to my eyes
to be stolen by my limbs
I am the horizon adorned with your lust.

In the night which withdraws like a mystic poppy to enter
the forest of limbs, we were—you and I—listening to a whisper
of trees, a breeze of arches
roads are cells of raw amber
there a feminine time gets into a masked dance
there virility oozes from a flower...

And you and I used to mumble
spices shudder
thorns bloom
we must dwell into another body
and reap our harvest
we must crush the civilization of language and cry out:
we are the two green wild animals
we clamor like a caress of the sea...

...Like dispatching nerves, our words were relayed between
    Kassiun
and *Jaramana*. Time within our bodies
was a wide earth aflame, and in our features grief built
    mountains and lakes.
But the earth was changing, the plowing was deeper.
Thus under the tree's reign, we proceeded,
guided by our faces revealing the shapes of the night.
And I saw your natural quietness
enter its beautiful destruction
I repeat:
in grief I give you my name
in exile I grow in you
trees, bend over us
fill us, O absence, do not be afraid...

IX

...A lustful touch
cells swept away
I exclude you from
how-why-where
and pursue my wonder.

A tipsy fluff
I add my *kohl* to your wine
and with you I move on towards a clamor
that drinks from my parts.

Fill her, O absence, do not be afraid
once more, the poet is hidden by divining clouds
breaking into rain
with a prophecy:
he will marry a cloud
he will never know where to seek shelter.
Say, O thunder: "his home is my home."

X

...Say his home is your home O thunder and choose your name:
Damascus—a millstone of atrocities forever imprinted on his
    days' memory
voices carrying the power of funerals
but here-now is your name divided in two,
and with the glory of your name
the poem is now resuming your flow
letter by letter:
you are the path to creativity
within poetry's range.
Resentful, he has hidden his unhealed wound from the city.
In its ebb, he often rolled but did not break,
in its stinginess and tepidity he endlessly dug and drilled
without being subdued.
How can you forbid yourself to me?
The poet says:
You are the radiance and he is your own reflection
you are every direction and each journey is to you.
Your body is a princely orchard heavy with taxation
and his heart cherishes the toll.
You are the leaven of all roads to passion
and utmost splendor
you are temptation
how can you forbid yourself to me, says the poet
how can we clash?

Haihat, haihat
inhabited towards you
wondering to you
entrusted to you by the wind.

TRANSFORMATIONS OF THE LOVER

Women are your garments and you are theirs.
　　　　　　The Holy Qur'an
The body is the dome of the soul.
　　　　　　St. Grégoire Palamas

I

Her name was walking silently through forests of letters
And letters were arches and velveteen animals
　　an army fighting with wings and tears.

The air was kneeling and the sky stretched out like hands.
Suddenly
Strange plants bloomed and the brook which stood behind the
　　forest drew near
I saw fruits clasped waist to waist like links in a chain
The flowers broke into dance
Forgetting their feet and fibers
Shielded by the shroud.

Joints, muscles, faces were the remains of a daylight's banquet
which had sickened and died
to guests whose names were not yet born...

(And I saw a procession of white horses riding the skies, so I
    hurtled on, screaming: "A snake
Is running after me." And I kept on screaming: "A snake
    as long as a
    a date palm.")
But the procession of horses rushed on and did not hear me.
    I said
I shall take a horse and be saved
I pleaded, and realized I had no voice.

I girded my loins to the winds of grief and dispersed
Behold—a sweet-scented old man is in my path.
I greeted him, I asked:
"Can you protect me from this snake?"
"I am weak and he is stronger than I. There is a protector on
    the road.
    Hurry."
I hurried until I reached the air
The sky approaching, I appeared and vanished in the dark
While the wind uttered and repeated me
I heard the old man's voice from a distance:
"There is a mountain before you filled
with the bounties of life. It holds something deposited for you
which will give you victory and refuge."
"Raise the curtains and come forth."

I turned and suddenly the mountain was windows
The windows were babies and mothers. Dumbfounded
    I looked:
    a crying girl
was saying this is my father, she then pointed to the snake and
    it fled,
A hand reached towards me
It drew me, and admitted me into a strange place, ancient
    and splendid
    as light.
There a bed awaited me. A phantom sitting at its head arose
Like a breast dressed in buttocks and bosom and the rest.

My body was aroused, falling captive to the pores and the rims
    of the eye
and the navel,
and that other nature which breeds different poppies
mandrakes and other female and male plants.

And my skin started to brace
for the fall of another star in its folds.

II

You grow in all directions
You grow towards the depths.

You open up to me like a spring
You surrender like a tree.

And I
I was suspended from the towers of the dream
I trace my forms around them
I invent secrets to fill the cracks of days.

I engraved your limbs with the embers of mine
I wrote you on my lips and my fingers
I carved you on my brow, altered the letters and the spellings
    I multiplied the readings.

My sighs were clouds bracing the horizon
I wove for you a robe tinted with sun
The night was a radiance which led me to you.

I hid in your garment's folds
I accompanied you to school

Our footsteps stole the threshold's bell.

And we slipped away
I sat to your left in class
I slept between your eyelashes.

But did not see you.

You were on a journey which had not reached us.

Your garments the climes; the seasons your path to me.

On tree trunks we read our names
With the stone we rolled
Trees are voices as we are, the earth beneath our blaze, is a fruit
We stroll with a cloud
We talk with the houses
The day walks behind us, covered with grass.

Then you rise, incense towards *Qasyun*
And I reel in your smoke
    Obedient, intimate, bearing your shy taste.

III

Liber, Libera, Phallus...

A thread of dawn, acrid to the eye, awakes us
A tread carrying people and mosses.

Shut your eyelids tight.

In our flesh, light raises its hills and banners
And the flame spreads from pillow to pillow.

Shut your eyelids tight
Daylight announces dusk—awaken.

To you
I trespass the vessel of my body
I discover the earth hidden in the map of sex
I advance.

Covering my path with talismans and signs
I obviate them with my bushy delirium, with fire and tattoos
I consider myself a wave and you the shore
Your back, a half-continent and under your breasts

my four winds.

I branch around you
And plummet, between you and my self, an eagle with a
    thousand wings.

I hear your delirious limbs
I hear the moan of your waist and the greeting of your hips.

Overwhelmed
I enter the desert of anxiety calling your name
Descending to the lower strata
In the presence of a contracted world
I behold fire and tears in a single basin.

I behold the city of wonder
My plight is intoxicated.

Thus says the lord the body.

Days of the year gather around me
I make them into houses and beds, enter every bed and house
I merge the moon and sun
The hour of love rises.

I plunge into a river which leads from you to another land

I hear strange words
They become gardens, stones, waves, waves
And flowers of celestial thorns.

Thus says the lord the body.

Oh woman written with the lover's pen
Go where you will between my limbs
Stop and speak:
    my body splits discharging its treasures.

Displace my fixed stars
Lie down under and over my cloud
In the depths of springs, the peaks of mountains
High high high.

Become my face emerging from every face

A sun which does not rise in the east nor set in the west
Do not wake and do not slumber...

I rise to you I descend to you
I join my deepest worries and their outermost
I stone the thorns with omens and stars:
        I wash them. I quell them
And I assault you with my heart.

I tell the whisper to let me roam through your every cell.

You set up your bed
Or spread out the earth
We plant the body's trees
We wrap ourselves in our voices
Until the hour of rekindling appears
The body is estranged
Transformation has touched it
    The joints' ache, the limbs' throb, the geometry of the
        muscles and the splendor of
the act
The body's landings,
its risings, its plains, its course, its curves
The land of the waist gorged with stars and half stars,
    smoldering white
volcanoes
Cataracts of headstrong desire.
Afterwards we seek shade in the abdomen's canopy
Where the planet of sex revolves
The metamorphosis is complete
Your breasts become night and day.

We rise
The besieged borders open
All that is captive is free.

We give way to the suns we had halted
Let them spread over all things
We see their light flower and bear fruit
The world suddenly stumbles upon us
While saying
The tree of the spirit has sprouted from the earth.

Thus says the lord the body.

IV

Liber, Libera, Phallus...
Love upon the sea, sea borne by the wind, wind borne by fate
    The weight of this world and what is upon it,
    two letters
    from the book of the body.

The body a dome borne by water unto the seventh earth
    There, we dwell with an army of giants
    and lovers of love.

"Woman, what have you seen?"
"A knight, saying: 'There is nothing you wish but shall be.'
    I took what wheat I had sown, and said unto it, rise, and it did.
    I said reap yourself
                  and it was reaped. I said
winnow yourself, and it was winnowed. I said mill yourself,
    and it
was milled. I said bake yourself, and it was baked.
And when I saw that all I had wished came to be, I feared
    and awoke,
upon a pillow."

"And you, O man, what have you seen?"
"A wind full of shooting stars herded by children"
"What else?"
"A moving hill breaking away from a pregnant gazelle"
"What else?"
"We were together in a ship, and you were pregnant. And
    while we
                            intimately embraced
the ship broke up, we were saved by a plank, upon which
you delivered your child."

You cried: "I am thirsty." And I said, "Where shall I find water,
    when such is
our plight?" I then lifted my gaze to the heavens and there
    was a phantom holding out a jug to me
I took it, gave you a drink
I drank
A water more desirable than honey
And I saw him vanish as he said, "I yielded my love to a
    lover's whims
    and was granted a home in the wind."

Liber, Libera, Phallus...
Untamed, my body is like the horizon, my limbs like date

palms
You bear fruit in me
Under your breast, I ripen, I dry, you are my hyssop and water
Each fruit is a wound and a path to you
I wade through you, you are my dwelling, I dwell in you, you
    are my waves,
Your body is a sea and every wave a sail
Your body is a spring and each crease a dove cooing my name.

You draw my limbs to your body
I am guided by pain and drunken pangs
I settle in it, replete with its east and west
I spread it, dust and a tomb
A kingdom I plunder and defend
I panic, I dare
I seek help in the forests and steppes
In the primal clay
In the nobility of panthers, the seclusion of eagles.

I am torn and broken descending to its depths
Full of creatures bursting into flames extinguished sighing
    moaning rising
    crazed
Sinking, kneeling

Distraught I enter a state of perplexity
I renounce the earth and approach it, alone, suspended by
    my soul
An abyss engulfs me
Opens and shuts its bowels on me.

    I hear an angel night-speaking with me, and waves cry out,
        "mount the bridge."
I mount descending to the depths,
Capsized.
Limbs quieting, I emerge and
Gather up my heart, scattered to the end of my frame
I return to the dream
I raise my eyes to you who calls me:
        "You tarried, my love, you tarried
        My body is a tent, you, you are its ropes and pegs
        You tarried, my love, you tarried..."

Liber, Libera, Phallus...
An infant beneath my garment cries love love
Tearfully, intoxicated
Weary he bears the path
    Trees are his lamp and the air his tower and bell
    His love races ahead of the wind
Flying into the limitless

towards the sky the sky the sky

I arrived
I saw the mountain a sea, and the sea enchanted trees
Your body is a city
      Rows upon rows of servants emerge from under the
        grottos of your
                            neck
      and the arch of your eyelids
And with my advance come the tidings
Every vulture a window
Every pulse a lover.

Dim translucent windows and doors are raised
Castles and gardens and squares glisten.

O woman you remember
Our house standing apart in a weave of olive and fig trees
And the spring sleeping round it, small as a pupil of the eye.

O woman you remember
The wood fluttering like moth
And night ushering the earth...

Night...
Deepen the chasms of your body, be the wild and embrace me
I will have a history of thunder
Plains plowed by departures
Tents and a lone litter
An island from the inkwells of the body
I reach its borders with my death and dwell in the beginnings
    of letters.

Night...

In feathers I erect my tent
I quiver
I prepare the tools of the journey
Each quiver a country, its roads as luminous as my guts
We bend we tauten we meet we part we mime
(You are my garment, I am yours)
Muscles ferment
Skin takes the color of violet, the taste of sea
Where the abyss beckons and our limbs set sail.

We hear the bed wailing
We glimpse our roots dressing in death.

We bend and lurch.

Water savior love
Why is fatigue restful
O web tighter than water
        O love?

Weddings weddings
Another magic illumines our faces
and not the sun
We plunge into a spring, wash off our dust.

Weddings, weddings
We offer them as sacrifice to take revenge on death.

A black god seeing all:
We are his flock in sleep and waking
In love and all that is not love.

Weddings weddings
We enfold our faces to enchanted cities
Open our borders to sex

And the dream is an earth rotating beneath our lashes.

O that other love within love
O dimension which begins beyond all others
O my love!

As I created you, you lusted for me
As I wished you, you poured into me.

You enter into my rhythm
    You anoint your breast with my words and drown in the
        depth of love
    where I erect my city and come to life
We live, and in the depth of hate, we proclaim love
We dream that our lashes are inkwells and the day an
    open book
Farther than the dream we journeyed
Farther than the heart we loved
To those who give names we said do not name us, We awak-
ened
    You are a lake
    and I a mandrake root sated with earth
I moor on your shores, and your waist is my anchor
Ah last woman, last lover.

What tide awaits us, what gulf?
My soul is locked like an oyster and you are my pearl and
    my angler
Your face bears my sail, Between our love and the sky
    the space is no more sufficient.

I uncover the other face of day
I behold the other face of night
I cry out to the sea: O untamable One, break like a reed
And to the thunder: listen!
      I ask:
Is love the only place which Death does not visit?
Can the mortal learn love?
And what shall I name you, O Death?

Between me and myself there comes a distance
    Where love lies in wait, where death lies in wait
And the body is my baptism.

From the depth of ephemeral things I proclaim love

Liber, Libera, Phallus...

V

"O man how did you wed me?"
"I was a wild outcast with no shelter
             to rest in
      I fell asleep and awakened.

   And behold there was a woman at my pillow
   And I remembered Eve and Adam's rib and knew you were
      my wife.

That day I dreamed that clouds were raised to me
And a voice called out: choose what you will
And I chose a black cloud; I drank from it, I gave you a drink
And I said
O body contract, expand, come forth, disappear
And it contracted, expanded, came forth, disappeared
And I saw my garments fall away from me
And darkness envelop me
And the world emerged from me screaming like a spear:
            'Go down deep deep in the dark'
And I fell into the dark
I saw the stone a light and the sand streaming waters
I encountered you and saw myself
And I said

I shall remain in the dark and never leave
But
The sun came and set me free
And I saw everything enter the sun...
      And how O woman did you wed me"?

"My body was a wind-swept to you
Colored by an earth swept to you

      O planet of stormy winds...."

VI

Yesterday
I bolted the door of my room with the first star
I lowered the only curtain and slept with her letters
And behold, my pillow was wet and the words pregnant.

I am a sorcerer and I name her incense and mortar
A sorcerer, and she my censer and altar in the starting embers
I stretch in the denseness of smoke
        Making the signs of magic
        Enchanting her wound
        Erasing the wound with my skin
O wound O incandescent Hell
O wound O intimate Death
In the wound are turrets and angels
A river locks its gate and grasses rove
A man strips
Crumbles hardened hyssop and howls
Then water drips upon his head
Then he bows and disappears.

I dream—
    I wash the earth until it becomes a mirror

I surround it with a wall of mist, a hedge of fire
I build a dome of tears, fashion it with my hands.

"What will you give me as a last gift?"
"My shirt which enveloped us on our wedding night. And
              I shall
    descend with you to the grave to ease for you
    the death of love
I mix you with my water and give you, a drink, to death
I give you my possessions: the grave and the gift of death."

 Once I saw her in a bottle on the ground
    A sea sweeping down
    Filled with oysters and other world dwellers turning into
    Birds and wings
And I said
    If woman's translucence could mingle with that of heavens'
    If the world could be a stone inhabited by sex
And I saw her a sea sweeping down
    Fell in love with the foam and dug for it a niche near
      my eye
    I vowed that the waves would be my neighbor
In their salt I walk my worries
Awake with me or dozing
Reading to me her echoes

She whispers (you are an angel who sees only beneath
    the skin
Your sole resemblance with the angel.

Do you wish, then, to uncover the continent of the deep?
    Leave
to another the discovery of the heights).

The deep...
(We were a great throng, women and men, walking the
    woman's path.
Suddenly a panther came upon us and blocked the way. I said
    to the
         man beside me
"Have we no knight to restrain this panther?"
"I do not know. But I know one woman who may"
"Where is she?"
    So he went, and I with him, to a nearby litter and called:
"Nada, come down and restrain this panther"
And she said:
"Would it please you that he looks upon me when he is male
    and I female?
Say to him: "Nada greets you and commands you to clear
    the path.""

So he went to the panther and said: "Nada greets you and
    commands
        you to clear the path."
And the panther bowed his head and vanished.)

The deep...
    Let me strike at life, let no wound hold me back
Why do you hasten my death, O dear ladies
Let me
    Let me hear bells in my memory and discover they are
        wombs and children
    Hear the world in the bells
    Where the sun becomes green in the water, white in
        the body
    Enters the orbit of the skull and borders the planet of
        the wound
Let me
    See my papers grow into narcissi and brooks
    See water become a book and the book celestial spheres
        and shores
    And see stars become dreams
    The dream a tree
    The tree a woman and a woman's future
    I lack another world to add new words to my language
    I lack Death

Let me
    See a body trickling seashells, seashells
    Seashells rounded like pillars
    Between one pillar and the next pregnant clouds are dying
       leaving children
           I do not know save the rain and the clover.

A grieving seashell summoned me and read to me her poem
She also read pages from her book "The Seashell's Chamber"
As she read she revealed her secrets:
    I saw an elephant emerge from the horn of a snail
    I saw camels and stallions in oysters the size of a butterfly
    A strange being was born before my very eyes, half stone
       and half animal
She pointed to it and whispered: "This is Woman."

She then whispered to me: "Place your ear between my papers."

O God
    I heard the rhythm of seasons
    I heard the music of a falling house, swelling with the fall
    And when I announced my departure I heard voices echo:
    "Peace be with the seashell, with the spiraled entry

Peace be with the king of mountains sleeping there
Peace be with his singing swallows..."

O Woman, lock up
My body is a locked room
My body is a forest, dams and locked canals.

Lock up
Our bodies are angles and narrow wrappings
Our bodies are a bolt, a latch   Access to us is
a disease of the plants rooted in the narrow clearing
Between our thighs and our eyes
A disease oozing gospels or madness.

Lock up
All our seashells shall remain locked, even if broken
All the eggs and their nests shall remain locked.

Lock up
Shut your lids tight
All our burst days burst, are driven into a locked year.

Lock up
The color of our lashes, when we are naked

And don our dreams and whisper
A stoppered vial...

VII

The lover's sun is suspended, bent by the sun
The concealed must take time off like harvest and planting
And my face must melt into the world's spirit.

Shall I rend the book of Exodus
Bend over my image and read its sand with scales like a coat
    of arms
Shall I whisper to my garment:
    Walk with a crutch as if dreaming while standing
    Hang in signs and banners
    In the forest of fingers and neck where, drunk and dizzy
    Like a sunflower?

Shall I say to this chair: Follow me but remain faithful to
    the fatigue
        steeped in pangs?
Shall I remind Death of the sheaves left behind after his last vis-
it?

Between me and my shells is a bow of distances and colors
Cities can pass under it and rest

My seashells also have their streets and trees, their bedrooms
and feasts.
If only the crab could speak I would ask him where he is
spending the night
If only the sea could sleep I would make its bed beside me...

1-Voice

"We leave both our heads outside the troth
We grant each its specter and addiction

Your head is a pillow, mine an erupting volcano."

We then write the deed:
    "Woman is a transient home for man, the transient one
    Man is the morrow of man, woman the future of woman."

With that we begin the following page:
    We speak with the feet
    With the ink and words of the pores
    We delight in their veiled passages
Suddenly
    Cinders erupt,   a thunderbolt beckons
    Awakening, each runs after his own head
    Yearning for dwelling and residence, for racing waves
    After that other homeland,
           the eternally lost...."

2-Conversation

"The body departs, its cannon remains, what shall you do
O love?"

"I will oppose the Earth."

3-Conversation

"Between you and me, a veil shields me from you
Where would you get initiative and discovery?
Death has fallen into your heart, let death illuminate you
But how would you violate the custom?

You beat, you blend...

My moods take no hold in you..."

"I am your lode
My sun has simmered you
I wore you as a signet, with which I sealed fate
I gird and remain free
I remove my finery for you
You wear me and I wear you..."

4-Song

The poet's body: A child's body and a raven's
Body in a book
In the chaff of curtains, in the door, in the vigilant stone
Between my eyes and the book.

Body in the corners
In the mirage which spawns underneath the mirrors.

Body withdrawing
A flying stone grazing or pelting the sky.

Body opening up in a dream, folding into the night,
    crumbling amidst
    the letters.

Body like letters
Body retreating to the first rows.

Body seeing itself
Like a suspended road, collapsing, opening its pages
    and questioning the sky

Where the echo knows not its role
Where there is nothing above my forthcoming stage
But the curtain and the echo.

5-Song

I summon you O End of Night exult and lengthen
Become a sorceress
On my bed
I summon you to say

"What shall love say to the lover
At the seasons' end?"

6-Song

Shahrayar is still
In the submissive bed, in the obedient room
In the mirrors of daylight
Keeping watch, sleepless, over disaster.

Light words stole his face
Taught him slumber
In the blackness of the lake, in the blueness of pebbles
Amid his familiar debris.

Shahrayar is still
Bearing his sword for the harvest
Clasping the wind's flask and ashes' vial.

Sheherazade forgot
To light the secret alleys
In the veins' orbit
She forgot to light the cracks
Between the face of the victim
And the footsteps of Shahrayar.

BODY
Excerpts

I

The earth was not a wound,

    it was a body/how can one travel between body and wound

how can one abide?

    O physicians O druggists O magicians and astrologers

                            O readers of absence

here I am practicing your secrets

    I change to an ostrich = I swallow tragedy's embers

        and digest the firestone of death/

I practice your secrets = I notice the absence of my facets

        breathless as if at home in my exile

        I am carried away = "my appearance is scattered I own
            nothing of it

        my inside burns I have no shade for it"

        and in one single moment

        I am dry I am dewy

I retreat I approach

I retreat I attack

humble I meditate/something is lodged between me and me

how can I incite my body to overcome me?

A rag from the jester's sun

Two lips attack his inner thighs, repeating/

a history which repeats itself

From here he has a glimpse of eternity

From here he senses the beginning

Eternity = Beginning

O pulse who rules over the invisible

Be his very rhythm

Grant his head to fall into your arms

He the stricken, the repentant

He the fresh water

He the temple which grants sperm and light.

II

His dwelling between trees and crops had the pallor of reeds,
　　drunkenness of wings

　　　　he made a pact with the waves

　　　　lured with the quietness of stone

　　　　convinced language to lie down as poppy's ink

the ladder we call time was leaning on his name

　　　　　　　　　　and climbing

　　　　　　　　　　from prophecy

　　　　　　　　　　to prophecy

　　　　from wings emerges ether

　　　　from coincidence emerges destiny

but

O sun O sun what do you want from me ?

　　　　a face gathers itself a lake/separates a swan

　　　　a chest trembles a skylark/rests a lotus

a basin opens up a flower/closes a pearl

these are the bushes of exile and desert's banners

the day is but a doll's hand

and the universe a clown's inflection

but

O sun O sun what do you want from me?

      Death is wearing a violet's beingness
      a narcissus dwells in snow's vessels dreaming that love
        is a face

                and it is its mirror.

      The stone is a bud, the cloud a butterfly

    and the body on the threshold—a spark to read the night

    Death is not to leave a body

      death is to leave what is not a body

but

O sun O sun what do you want from me?

      hurdles outnumber me

veils make me more radiant/

I breath the abyssal plant, find nothing but cages between
my feet.

If the cages catch fire, if time were a bush

and the bush, a woman

if the sky undid its buttons

I would be cured of the "I wish and if only"

and I would tell the sky, burst forth in search

of a second motherhood,

free your eyelashes from tears

yield to another water

you are neither dream nor eyes

you are no wisdom to me/my wisdom lies in the wind bearing
the fruit

that nourishes my days

and whose ships move away the shore.

But

how does an anchoring line rest when guarding the waves
    and you

O sun O sun what do you want from me?

      I seek that which does not find me

      In its name I sink, a rose to the wind

         North and South, East and West

     to which I add depth and height

    But which way do I turn?

    My eyes are the color of a slice of bread

    and my body falls toward a disease as pure as fluff

       neither can love reach me

       nor hate get to me

but

which way do I turn? O sun O sun what do you want from me?

III

He erases his face/discovers his face

an impulse comes forth   you are wrapped in temptation's
     first dawn

          time comes forth   where is that space in
               which life becomes temporal?

darkness comes forth   which tremor will distribute you to
     my blood

               I say you are the climate, the rotation and
                    the sphere

               which upheaval

light comes forth   it darkens my parts

                    I break and connect

                    while time puts on a skin's complexion

                         and steps out of time

                    and your conquest

                    falls

upon me

and I burst out sobbing to you.

Why did you conquer me

and when you came in, why did the fields ignite, my hands the
first fire

and why

each night

did I carry your breast's fluff into the coming night?

Enter

With dirt on your knees, and on the road to you—to
me mountains

and the cypresses of slopes

and the valley's pines/I say we meet—we separate

I gather my parts

O colocynth, whose bitterness spreads like salt

you are sweetness itself and to you I grant my first taste.

                                    Enter

we meet we separate/separation has no wings nor meeting
    an umbra

I hide inside my features

you hide between your breasts—

        Mix us O bend

        a body that soars

        a body that submits

        and bless us

the notebook of means is complete

migration's cases are now open

        your body is a maze/I depart

        to you, my exodus.

I take you, a land I do not know

hills and valleys covered by plants intent on discovery

obscure plains inhabited by sand

> brown yellow blue

inhabited by time/its pebbles and crushed stones are

rows of hills like rows of wheat

> slanting and narrowing

fields spread with down sheathing flint

heights wrapped in clouds oblivious of sun

ridges blazing with a sun oblivious of clouds/a land I do
not know

and I take you standing

sitting

reclining

and yield to none but you/

> I take you

in my sighs

in waking and in sleep

and in the trances between

I take you

in what time holds for me

I take you

crease after crease

and invent my paths.

I stretch in you I do not reach

I circle I do not reach

I thread and weave myself and still do not reach

I reach out of your very depth and do not reach

beyond all distances beyond all deserts

you

where whether what how and when and you

are not you/

Spread out over my body and sink

cell within a cell

vein within a vein

take root/

    let thousands of lips sprout from you

    thousands of teeth

  let them be anonymous to measure with our love

this that while

    a member is driven insane

    a member is ecstatic

and in the creases of our hips a trickle of water

  spreads out over you/over me and abates

but I already have linked your image with all images

seen the light and said

        this is our last encounter

        O woman who are you?

I take you O man

  heavenly animal

    spreading poison with one lip

      a balm with the other

and each night I say

this is our first encounter

One

M

O

O

N

IRIDESCENT

I want nothing from you but cooings

nothing but sparkles

and all that wanders

my body shivers in its required substance

in its very faculties

and I scream: you are the dust

you are the power/

who are you?

A body grows between the lavender and the immortelle

it falls, rises, looms

assembles the shores and probes the rambling of reeds/

    I touched you with my eyes

    a dance advancing in the seasons' footsteps

    I inhaled the valerian

    and shapes started to roam the abyss of

    the hip—the drowned clashing with the drowned

        I get out of the reed

enter the flower

sneak into the hiding of its base

    where eggs lie and where signs come to an end

    I gather the way pollen gathers/I undress you/I adorn
        myself with you.

I snatch myself from you/I cling to you

    between you and me I create

        a lie as high as the sun

        a duplicity which breaks time

        branch after branch/

O woman   who are you?

.....

a patch from the buffoon's sun—

    O man you once said:

    put me in your body's coffers and store me

    your body is a water lily, mine a lake/

    a dip or a drowning

    a tilt or a fall?

And you said:

O you, thrown, shore after shore, over the range of our passion,

O ship—break free

    the alga may peel

    the depth of secrets may burn

where the echo covers the deep—break free

    breaking free is the very church of bodies

and the body is madness's priest.

And you said:

hand in hand/heart upon heart

goes the body and the hurricane—neither the storm subsides

nor the skin is protected

let the body go mad, a madness which takes over understanding

let the wind go mad, the ocean's madness

and you said:

how can pebbles praise in one's hands

and water gush between the fingers?

and you said:

I appeal to my time for a delay so I can become a verse which
    speaks in the name of

love

and you said:

it is the body which wounds life—which transplants and exiles

the body which becomes liquid, takes the vessel's shape

and you said:

the body, not love, is the skin of time, the earth's pores

the body, not love, is the horizon's arch and the wind's muscles/

would you like to understand?

then ignore who you are

ignore the other.

And you said:

I have mixed and twisted

I have spread my voice, dislocated my words

I have sheathed the language

and you cried:

O Man

who was born sick

when will you recover?

IV

Enter/my parts are aching

towards you/I have plundered you

ripened in you

anchored my moods

enter/let us meet = separate/erase our faces—discover our faces

mix bread with wounds to keep the earth under our words

to retain the courage of refusal, to write a different history

see a woman-lake/a river-lover

while our bodies drift

and we rise like arches/and slip in the universe.

Naked

the universe leaves its home, comes down our steps

we bathe in the thundering of things

moments hide lions which are pleasurable

    we are country and city

    we are scattered and disciplined

we are familiar and different

things have no name

    things have legs like stags

        faces like lovers

        and here is space

                a white fur

and pillows smell of luxurious bushes

    and here is the body—the father/the body—the mother

        steering ahead.

We steer

greeted by the bells of desire

greeted by beds as high as childhood, as candid as the sun

we invent a death as long as life

we invent a duplicity

    between you and me

    a lie

which snaps at time branch after branch/

We meet=we separate=erase our faces=discover our faces/

in the bed two phantasms

one which views/one which hides

and the two bodies are four

    half for the present

    half for the absent/

an army of needles strikes at our guts

the body we sound gives us no shelter

but cracks revealing what they hide

and lines which read to us primordial secrets/

How can a single body bear jasmine and boxthorn

how can a single heart wear two bodies?

We agree—we disagree

we invent a deception as high as childhood

    a lie as candid as the sun

we invent a death as long as life

and say

    love is threesome—a man and a man and a woman

      a man and a woman and a woman

    always

    there was

    between us

    a distance—   we said

the blaze we call love will erase it

but days stuck to days and nights to nights and still between us
the distance remained

we extinguished that which cannot be extinguished

we ignited the unignitable

still the distance between us remained

and in the hours of soldering screams with screams and sperm
with sperm

between us the distance remained.

O love, O extinguished birth

    come forth and sit on my knees—on our knees

    take the needle of tears and weave the water

the bells of desire greet us

we invent a death as long as life

we invent a deception as high as childhood

a lie as candid as the sun/

        who are we?

a bridge we cannot cross brings us together

a wall unites and separates us/I enter you I leave myself

    I leave you I enter myself—

        that which I build destroys me.

Notes on the Translations

Translations by Mirène Ghossein:

Translations by Kamal Boullata:

Translations by Kamal Boullata and Mirène Ghossein:

Translations by Kamal Boullata and Susan Einbinder:

Sources of the Poems

From *Qasa'id Ula* (First Poems), al Maktabah al-'Asriyya, Beirut, 1963: "Love" (January 1989); and "The House of Love," pp. 106-108.

From *Kitab al-Tahawwulat wal-Hijra fi Aqalim al-Layl wal-Nahar* (The Book of Changes and Migration in the Regions of Night and Day), al-Maktabah al-'Asriyya, Beirut, 1965: "Transformations of the Lover," pp. 113-166.

From *Waqt Bayn al-Ramad wal-Ward* (Time Between Ash and Roses), Manshurat Mawaqif, Beirut, 1970: "I Give Myself to the Abyss of Sex," pp. 39-69.

From *al-Masrah wal-Maraya* (The Stage and the Mirrors) in Complete Works Vol. II, Dar al-'Awdah, 2nd edition, Beirut, 1971: "A Mirror for Khalida," pp. 484-488.

From *Mufrad bi Sighat al-Jam'* (Singular in the Form of Plural), Dar al-'Awdah, Beirut, 1975: "Body," pp. 125-139.

From *Mawaqif*, No. 30-31 (Winter/Spring), Beirut, 1975: "Beginning of Words," p. 129.

From *Kitab al-Qasa'id al-Khams* (The Books of the Five Poems), Dar al-'Awdah, Beirut, 1980: "Qays," p. 169;

Bibliography

POETRY

Qasa'id Ula (First Poems), 1957, 1963, 1970

Awraq fil-Rih (Leaves in the Wind), 1958, 1959, 1970

Aghani Mihyar al-Dimashqi (Songs of Mihyar the Dama-
scene) 1961, 1970, 1971

*Kitab al-Tahawwulat wal-Hijra fi Aqalim al-Layl wal-Na-
har* (The Book of Changes and Migrations in the Re-
gions of Night and Day), 1965, 1970

al-Masrah wal-Maraya (The Stage and the Mirrors), 1968

Waqt Bay al-Ramad wal-Ward (Time Between Ashes and
Roses), 1970, 1971

al-Athar al-Shi'riyya al-Kamila (Complete Works), 2 vol-
umes, 1971

Mufrad bi Sighat al-Jam' (Singular in the Form of Plural),
1977

Kitab al-Qasa'id al-Khams (The Book of the Five Poems),
1980

Kitab al-Hisar (The Book of Siege), 1985

CRITICAL WRITING

Muqaddama lil-Shi'r al-'Arabi (An Introduction to Arabic
Poetry), 1971

Zaman al-Shi'r (A Time for Poetry), 1972

al-Thabit wal-Mutahawwil (Immobility and Change), 3
    volumes, 1974, 1977, 1978, 1979

Fatiha li Nihayat al-Qarn (Preface to the End of the Cen-
    tury), 1980

Siyasat al-Shi'r (The Politics of Poetry), 1984

al-Shi'riyya al-'Arabiyya (Arabic Poetics), 1985

TRANSLATIONS FROM THE FRENCH

Complete Works of George Shihadeh:

Histoire de Vasco (Hikayat Vasco), 1972

Monsieur Boble (al-Sayyed Bobel), 1972

L'émigré de Brisbane (al-Muhajir min Brisban), 1973

La Violette (al-Banafsaj), 1973

Le Voyage (al-Safar), 1975

La Soirée de Proverbes (Saharat al-Amthal), 1975

Complete Works of St. John Perse:

Amers (Minarat), 1976

Exil, Anabase, Eloges, La Gloire des Rois, L'amitie du Prince
    (Manfa was Qasa'id Ukhra), 1978

Plays by Racine:

Thèbes ou les Deux Frères Ennemis (Ma'sat Tiba aw al-

Shaqiqan al-'Aduwwan), 1979

Phèdre (Fedra), 1979

GREEN INTEGER
Pataphysics and Pedantry

Edited by Per Bregne
Douglas Messerli, *Publisher*

Essays, Manifestos, Statements, Speeches, Maxims,
Epistles, Diaristic Notes, Narratives, Natural Histories,
Poems, Plays, Performances, Ramblings, Revelations
and all such ephemera as may appear necessary
to bring society into a slight tremolo of confusion
and fright at least.

*

Green Integer Books

Green Integer EL-E-PHANT Books (6 x 9 format)